The Inner Voice of Love

Henri J. M. Nouwen

IMAGE BOOKS

DOUBLEDAY

New York   London   Toronto   Sydney   Auckland

The

Inner

Voice

of

Love

A Journey Through

Anguish to Freedom

AN IMAGE BOOK
PUBLISHED BY DOUBLEDAY
a division of Random House, Inc.
1540 Broadway, New York, New York 10036

IMAGE, DOUBLEDAY, and the portrayal of a deer drinking
from a stream are trademarks of Doubleday, a division of
Random House, Inc.

First Image Books edition published February 1998 by special
arrangement with Doubleday.
The Library of Congress has cataloged the hardcover edition
of this book as follows:

Nouwen, Henri J. M.
The inner voice of love: a journey through
anguish to freedom / Henri J. M. Nouwen.—
1st ed.
p. cm.
I. Nouwen, Henri J. M.—Diaries.   2. Catholic
Church—Clergy—Diaries.   3. Distress
(Psychology)   4. Anxiety—Religious
aspects—Christianity.
5. Spiritual life—Christianity.
I. Title.
BX4705.N87A3   1996
282.092—dc20   96-8162
CIP

30

To Wendy and Jay Greer

Contents

Acknowledgments . . . . *xi*

Introduction . . . . *xiii*

A Suggestion to the Reader . . . . *xxi*

Work Around Your Abyss 3

Cling to the Promise 4

Stop Being a Pleaser 5

Trust the Inner Voice 6

Cry Inward 7

Always Come Back to the Solid Place 8

Set Boundaries to Your Love 9

Give Gratuitously 11

Come Home 12

Understand the Limitations of Others 13

Trust in the Place of Unity 14

Remain Attentive to Your Best Intuitions 16

Bring Your Body Home 19

Enter the New Country 21

Keep Living Where God Is 23

Rely on Your Spiritual Guides 25

Go into the Place of Your Pain 26

Open Yourself to the First Love 28

Acknowledge Your Powerlessness 30

Seek a New Spirituality 32

Tell Your Story in Freedom 34

Find the Source of Your Loneliness 36

Keep Returning to the Road to Freedom 38

Let Jesus Transform You 40

Befriend Your Emotions 42

Follow Your Deepest Calling 44

Remain Anchored in Your Community 45

Stay with Your Pain 47

Live Patiently with the "Not Yet" 49

Keep Moving Toward Full Incarnation 51

See Yourself Truthfully 53

Receive All the Love That Comes to You 55

Stay United with the Larger Body 57

Love Deeply 59

Stand Erect in Your Sorrow 61

Let Deep Speak to Deep 63

Allow Yourself to Be Fully Received 65

Claim Your Unique Presence in Your
Community 67

Accept Your Identity as a Child of God 70

Own Your Pain 72

Know Yourself as Truly Loved 74

Protect Your Innocence 76

Let Your Lion Lie Down with Your Lamb . . . 78

Be a Real Friend 80

Trust Your Friends   82

Control Your Own Drawbridge   84

Avoid All Forms of Self-Rejection   86

Take Up Your Cross   88

Keep Trusting God's Call   89

Claim the Victory   91

Face the Enemy   93

Continue Seeking Communion   95

Separate the False Pains from the Real Pain . . .   97

Say Often, "Lord, Have Mercy"   98

Let God Speak Through You   99

Know That You Are Welcome   101

Permit *Your* Pain to Become *the* Pain   103

Give Your Agenda to God   105

Let Others Help You Die   107

Live Your Wounds Through   109

For Now, Hide Your Treasure   111

Keep Choosing God   113

Conclusion   116

Acknowledgments

Connie Ellis was the first person who typed the manuscript of this book, and Conrad Wieczorek was the first person who edited it. Both have since died. I remember them with much affection and gratitude.

Kathy Christie, my secretary, and Susan Brown, my editor, have done a great deal to make this text ready for publication. I thank them both for their caring and competent work.

A special word of gratitude goes to my friend Wendy Greer, who encouraged me during the past three years to overcome my hesitation to publish this book and offered many good ideas for changes and corrections. The generous financial support of Wendy and her husband, Jay, and their many friends has been a great source of inspiration to me.

I also want to thank Alice Allen and Ed Goebels for helping me with all the contractual work necessary for this publication.

Finally, many thanks to Bill Barry and Trace Murphy at Doubleday for their visits to me at the Daybreak community, for their continued interest in my writing, especially in this book, and for their flexibility and patience during the preparation of the final manuscript.

Introduction

This book is my secret journal. It was written during the most difficult period of my life, from December 1987 to June 1988. That was a time of extreme anguish, during which I wondered whether I would be able to hold on to my life. Everything came crashing down—my self-esteem, my energy to live and work, my sense of being loved, my hope for healing, my trust in God . . . everything. Here I was, a writer about the spiritual life, known as someone who loves God and gives hope to people, flat on the ground and in total darkness.

What had happened? I had come face to face with my own nothingness. It was as if all that had given my life meaning was pulled away and I could see nothing in front of me but a bottomless abyss.

The strange thing was that this happened shortly after I had found my true home. After many years of life in universities, where I never felt fully at home, I had become a member of L'Arche, a community of men and women with mental disabilities. I had been received with open arms, given all the attention and affection I could ever hope for, and offered a safe and loving place to grow spiritually as well as emotionally. Everything seemed ideal. But precisely at that time I fell apart—as if I needed a safe place to hit bottom!

Just when all those around me were assuring me they loved me, cared for me, appreciated me, yes, even admired me, I experienced myself as a useless, unloved, and despicable person. Just when people were putting their arms around me, I saw the endless depth of my human misery and felt that there was nothing worth living for. Just when I had found a home, I felt absolutely homeless. Just when I was being praised for my spiritual insights, I felt devoid of faith. Just when people were thanking me for bringing them closer to God, I felt that God had abandoned me. It was as if the house I had finally found had no floors. The anguish completely paralyzed me. I could no longer sleep. I cried uncontrollably for hours. I could not be reached by consoling words or arguments. I no longer had any interest in other people's problems. I lost all appetite for food and could not appreciate the beauty of music, art, or even nature. All had become darkness. Within me there was one long scream coming from a place I didn't know existed, a place full of demons.

All of this was triggered by the sudden interruption of a friendship. Going to L'Arche and living with very vulnerable people, I had gradually let go of many of my inner guards and opened my heart more fully to others. Among my many friends, one had been able to touch me in a way I had never been touched before. Our friendship encouraged me to allow myself to be loved and cared for with greater trust and confidence. It was a totally new experience for me, and it brought immense joy and peace. It seemed as if a door of my interior life had been opened, a door that had remained locked during my youth and most of my adult life.

But this deeply satisfying friendship became the road to my anguish, because soon I discovered that the enormous space that had been opened for me could not be filled by the one who had opened it. I became possessive, needy, and dependent, and when the friendship finally had to be interrupted, I fell apart. I felt abandoned, rejected, and betrayed. Indeed, the extremes touched each other.

Intellectually I knew that no human friendship

could fulfill the deepest longing of my heart. I knew that only God could give me what I desired. I knew that I had been set on a road where nobody could walk with me but Jesus. But all this knowledge didn't help me in my pain.

I realized quite soon that it would be impossible to survive this mentally and spiritually debilitating anguish without leaving my community and surrendering myself to people who would be able to lead me to a new freedom. Through a unique grace, I found the place and the people to give me the psychological and spiritual attention I needed. During the six months that followed, I lived through an agony that seemed never to end. But the two guides who were given to me did not leave me alone and kept gently moving me from one day to the next, holding on to me as parents hold a wounded child.

To my surprise, I never lost the ability to write. In fact, writing became part of my struggle for survival. It gave me the little distance from myself that I needed to keep from drowning in my despair. Nearly every day, usually immediately after meeting with my guides, I wrote a "spiritual imperative"—a command to myself that had emerged from our session. These imperatives were directed to my own heart. They were not meant for anyone but myself.

In the first weeks it seemed as if my anguish only got worse. Very old places of pain that had been hidden to me were opened up, and fearful experiences from my early years were brought to consciousness. The interruption of friendship forced me to enter the basement of my soul and look directly at what was hidden there, to choose, in the face of it all, not death but life. Thanks to my attentive and caring guides, I was able day by day to take very small steps toward life. I could easily have become bitter, resentful, depressed, and suicidal. That this did not happen was the result of the struggle expressed in this book.

When I returned to my community, not without great apprehension, I reread all I had written during the time of my "exile." It seemed so intense and raw that I could hardly imagine it would speak to anyone but me. Even though Bill Barry, a friend and a publisher at Doubleday, felt strongly that my most personal struggle could be of great help to many people, I was too close to it to give it away. Instead I started work on a book about Rembrandt's painting *The Return of the Prodigal Son* and found there a safe place for some of the insights I had gained from my struggles.

But when, eight years later, prompted by my friend Wendy Greer, I read my secret journal again, I was able to look back at that period of my life and see it as a time of intense purification that had led me gradually to a new inner freedom, a new hope, and a new creativity. The "spiritual imperatives" I had put down now seemed less private and even possibly of some value to others. Wendy and several other friends encouraged me not to hide this painful experience from those who have come to know me through my various books on the spiritual life. They reminded me that the books I had written since my period of anguish could not have been written without the experience I had gained by living through that time. They asked, "Why keep this away from those who have been nurtured by your spiritual insights? Isn't it important for your friends close by and far away to know the high cost of these insights? Wouldn't they find it a source of consolation to see that light and darkness, hope and despair, love and fear are never very far from each other, and that spiritual freedom often requires a fierce spiritual battle?"

Their questions finally convinced me to give these pages to Bill Barry and make them available in this book. I hope and pray that I did the right thing.

A Suggestion to the Reader

Do not read too many of these spiritual imperatives at once! They were written over a long period of
time and need to be read that way too. They also do
not need to be read in the order in which they ap-
pear. The table of contents gives you an idea of
which pages might be most helpful to you. These
spiritual imperatives are meant to be like salt for the
meal of your life. Too much salt might spoil it, but a
little at a time can make it tasty!

The Inner Voice of Love

Work Around Your Abyss

There is a deep hole in your being, like an abyss. You will never succeed in filling that hole, because your needs are inexhaustible. You have to work around it so that gradually the abyss closes.

Since the hole is so enormous and your anguish so deep, you will always be tempted to flee from it. There are two extremes to avoid: being completely absorbed in your pain and being distracted by so many things that you stay far away from the wound you want to heal.

Cling to the Promise

Do not tell everyone your story. You will only end up feeling more rejected. People cannot give you what you long for in your heart. The more you expect from people's response to your experience of abandonment, the more you will feel exposed to ridicule.

You have to close yourself to the outside world so you can enter your own heart and the heart of God through your pain. God will send to you the people with whom you can share your anguish, who can lead you closer to the true source of love.

God is faithful to God's promises. Before you die, you will find the acceptance and the love you crave. It will not come in the way you expect. It will not follow your needs and wishes. But it will fill your heart and satisfy your deepest desire. There is nothing to hold on to but this promise. Everything else has been taken away from you. Cling to that naked promise in faith. Your faith will heal you.

Stop Being a Pleaser

You have to let your father and father figures go. You must stop seeing yourself through their eyes and trying to make them proud of you.

For as long as you can remember, you have been a pleaser, depending on others to give you an identity. You need not look at that only in a negative way. You wanted to give your heart to others, and you did so quickly and easily. But now you are being asked to let go of all these self-made props and trust that God is enough for you. You must stop being a pleaser and reclaim your identity as a free self.

Trust the Inner Voice

Do you really want to be converted? Are you willing to be transformed? Or do you keep clutching your old ways of life with one hand while with the other you beg people to help you change?

Conversion is certainly not something you can bring about yourself. It is not a question of willpower. You have to trust the inner voice that shows the way. You *know* that inner voice. You turn to it often. But after you have heard with clarity what you are asked to do, you start raising questions, fabricating objections, and seeking everyone else's opinion. Thus you become entangled in countless often contradictory thoughts, feelings, and ideas and lose touch with the God in you. And you end up dependent on all the people you have gathered around you.

Only by attending constantly to the inner voice can you be converted to a new life of freedom and joy.

Cry Inward

A split between divinity and humanity has taken place in you. With your divinely endowed center you know God's will, God's way, God's love. But your humanity is cut off from that. Your many human needs for affection, attention, and consolation are living apart from your divine sacred space. Your call is to let these two parts of yourself come together again.

You have to move gradually from crying outward—crying out for people who you think can fulfill your needs—to crying inward to the place where you can let yourself be held and carried by God, who has become incarnate in the humanity of those who love you in community. No one person can fulfill all your needs. But the community can truly hold you. The community can let you experience the fact that, beyond your anguish, there are human hands that hold you and show you God's faithful love.

Always Come Back to the Solid Place

You must believe in the yes that comes back when you ask, "Do you love me?" You must *choose* this yes even when you do not experience it.

You feel overwhelmed by distractions, fantasies, the disturbing desire to throw yourself into the world of pleasure. But you know already that you will not find there an answer to your deepest question. Nor does the answer lie in rehashing old events, or in guilt or shame. All of that makes you dissipate yourself and leave the rock on which your house is built.

You have to trust the place that is solid, the place where you can say yes to God's love even when you do not feel it. Right now you feel nothing except emptiness and the lack of strength to choose. But keep saying, "God loves me, and God's love is enough." You have to choose the solid place over and over again and return to it after every failure.

Set Boundaries to
Your Love

When people show you their boundaries ("I can't do this for you"), you feel rejected. You cannot accept the fact that others are unable to do for you all that you expect from them. You desire boundless love, boundless care, boundless giving.

Part of your struggle is to set boundaries to your own love—something you have never done. You give whatever people ask of you, and when they ask for more, you give more, until you find yourself exhausted, used, and manipulated. Only when you are able to set your own boundaries will you be able to acknowledge, respect, and even be grateful for the boundaries of others.

In the presence of the people you love, your needs grow and grow, until those people are so overwhelmed by your needs that they are practically forced to leave you for their own survival.

The great task is to claim yourself for yourself, so that you can contain your needs within the boundaries of your self and hold them in the presence of those you love. True mutuality in love requires people who possess themselves and who can give to each other while holding on to their own identities. So, in order both to give more effectively and to be more self-contained with your needs, you must learn to set boundaries to your love.

Give Gratuitously

Your love, insofar as it is from God, is permanent. You can claim the permanence of your love as a gift from God. And you can give that permanent love to others. When others stop loving you, you do not have to stop loving them. On a human level, changes might be necessary, but on the level of the divine, you can remain faithful to your love.

One day you will be free to give gratuitous love, a love that does not ask for anything in return. One day also you will be free to receive gratuitous love. Often love is offered to you, but you do not recognize it. You discard it because you are fixed on receiving it from the same person to whom you gave it.

The great paradox of love is that precisely when you have claimed yourself as God's beloved child, have set boundaries to your love, and thus contained your needs, you begin to grow into the freedom to give gratuitously.

Come Home

There are two realities to which you must cling. First, God has promised that you will receive the love you have been searching for. And second, God is faithful to that promise.

So stop wandering around. Instead, come home and trust that God will bring you what you need. Your whole life you have been running about, seeking the love you desire. Now it is time to end that search. Trust that God will give you that all-fulfilling love and will give it in a human way. Before you die, God will offer you the deepest satisfaction you can desire. Just stop running and start trusting and receiving.

Home is where you are truly safe. It is where you can receive what you desire. You need human hands to hold you there so you don't run away again. But when you come home and stay home, you will find the love that will bring rest to your heart.

Understand the Limitations
of Others

You keep listening to those who seem to reject you.
But they never speak about *you*. They speak about
their own limitations. They confess their poverty in
the face of your needs and desires. They simply ask
for your compassion. They do not say that you are
bad, ugly, or despicable. They say only that you are
asking for something they cannot give and that they
need to get some distance from you to survive emotionally. The sadness is that you perceive their necessary withdrawal as a rejection of you instead of as a
call to return home and discover there your true
belovedness.

Trust in the Place
of Unity

You are called to live out of a new place, beyond your emotions, passions, and feelings. As long as you live amid your emotions, passions, and feelings, you will continue to experience loneliness, jealousy, anger, resentment, and even rage, because those are the most obvious responses to rejection and abandonment.

You have to trust that there is another place, to which your spiritual guides want to lead you and where you can be safe. Maybe it is wrong to think about this new place as *beyond* emotions, passions, and feelings. *Beyond* could suggest that these human sentiments are absent there. Instead, try thinking about this place as the core of your being—your heart, where all human sentiments are held together in truth. From this place you can feel, think, and act truthfully.

It is quite understandable that you are afraid of this place. You have so little knowledge of it. You have caught glimpses of it, you have even been there at times, but for most of your life you have dwelt among your emotions, passions, and feelings and searched in them for inner peace and joy.

Also, you have not fully acknowledged this new place as the place where God dwells and holds you. You fear that this truthful place is in fact a bottomless pit where you will lose all you have and are. Do not be afraid. Trust that the God of life wants to embrace you and give you true safety.

You might consider this the place of unification, where you can become one. Right now you experience an inner duality; your emotions, passions, and feelings seem separate from your heart. The needs of your body seem separate from your deeper self. Your thoughts and dreams seem separate from your spiritual longing.

You are called to unity. That is the good news of the Incarnation. The Word becomes flesh, and thus a new place is made where all of you and all of God can dwell. When you have found that unity, you will be truly free.

Remain Attentive to Your Best Intuitions

You are living through an unusual time. You see that you are called to go toward solitude, prayer, hidden-ness, and great simplicity. You see that, for the time being, you have to be limited in your movements, sparing with phone calls, and careful in letter writing.

You also know that the fulfillment of your burning desire for intimate friendships, shared ministry, and creative work will not bring you what you really want. It is a new experience for you to feel both the desire and its unreality. You sense that nothing but God's love can fulfill your deepest need while the pull to other people and things remains strong. It seems that peace and anguish exist side by side in you, that you desire both distraction and prayerful concentration.

Trust the clarity with which you see what you have to do. The thought that you may have to live away from friends, busy work, newspapers, and exciting books no longer scares you. It no longer gives rise to anxiety about what others will think, say, or do. Even the idea that you may soon be forgotten and lose your connections with the world does not upset you.

You find prayer quite easy. What a grace! People around you are going to the theater, ballet classes, or dinner parties, and you do not feel rejected or abandoned when they do not invite you to join them. In fact, you are very happy to be alone in your room. It is not hard to speak to Jesus and listen to him speaking to you. You are becoming aware of how close Jesus is to you. He holds you safe in his love. At times, memories of past events and fantasies about the future pierce your heart, but these painful incidents have become less frightening, less devastating, less paralyzing. It almost seems as if they are necessary reminders of your need to stay close—very close—to Jesus.

You know that something totally new, truly unique, is happening within you. It is clear that something in you is dying and something is being born. You must remain attentive, calm, and obedient to your best intuitions. You keep asking yourself, "What about the ways I have done and said things in the past? What about my many options in the future?" Suddenly you realize that these questions are no longer meaningful. In the new life you are entering, they won't be raised anymore. The stage sets that have for so long provided a background for your thoughts, words, and actions are slowly being rolled away, and you know they won't come back.

You feel a strange sadness. An enormous loneliness emerges, but you are not frightened. You feel vulnerable but safe at the same time. Jesus is where you are, and you can trust that he will show you the next step.

Bring Your Body Home

You have never felt completely safe in your body. But God wants to love you in all that you are, spirit and body. Increasingly, you have come to see your body as an enemy that has to be conquered. But God wants you to befriend your body so that it can be made ready for the Resurrection. When you do not fully own your body, you cannot claim it for an everlasting life.

How then do you bring your body home? By letting it participate in your deepest desire to receive and offer love. Your body needs to be held and to hold, to be touched and to touch. None of these needs is to be despised, denied, or repressed. But you have to keep searching for your body's deeper need, the need for genuine love. Every time you are able to go beyond the body's superficial desires for love, you are bringing your body home and moving toward integration and unity.

In Jesus, God took on human flesh. The Spirit of God overshadowed Mary, and in her all enmity between spirit and body was overcome. Thus God's Spirit was united with the human spirit, and the human body became the temple destined to be lifted up into the intimacy of God through the Resurrection. Every human body has been given a new hope, of belonging eternally to the God who created it. Thanks to the Incarnation, you can bring your body home.

Enter the New Country

You have an idea of what the new country looks like. Still, you are very much at home, although not truly at peace, in the old country. You know the ways of the old country, its joys and pains, its happy and sad moments. You have spent most of your days there. Even though you know that you have not found there what your heart most desires, you remain quite attached to it. It has become part of your very bones.

Now you have come to realize that you must leave it and enter the new country, where your Beloved dwells. You know that what helped and guided you in the old country no longer works, but what else do you have to go by? You are being asked to trust that you will find what you need in the new country. That requires the death of what has become so precious to you: influence, success, yes, even affection and praise.

Trust is so hard, since you have nothing to fall back on. Still, trust is what is essential. The new country is where you are called to go, and the only way to go there is naked and vulnerable.

It seems that you keep crossing and recrossing the border. For a while you experience a real joy in the

new country. But then you feel afraid and start longing again for all you left behind, so you go back to
the old country. To your dismay, you discover that
the old country has lost its charm. Risk a few more
steps into the new country, trusting that each time
you enter it, you will feel more comfortable and be
able to stay longer.

Keep Living Where God Is

When you experience a great need for human affection, you have to ask yourself whether the circumstances surrounding you and the people you are with are truly where God wants you to be. Whatever you are doing—watching a movie, writing a book, giving a presentation, eating, or sleeping—you have to stay in God's presence. If you feel a great loneliness and a deep longing for human contact, you have to be extremely discerning. Ask yourself whether this situation is truly God-given. Because where God wants you to be, God holds you safe and gives you peace, even when there is pain.

To live a disciplined life is to live in such a way that you want only to be where God is with you. The more deeply you live your spiritual life, the easier it will be to discern the difference between living with God and living without God, and the easier it will be to move away from the places where God is no longer with you.

The great challenge here is faithfulness, which must be lived in the choices of every moment. When your eating, drinking, working, playing, speaking, or writing is no longer for the glory of God, you should stop it immediately, because when you no longer live for the glory of God, you begin living for your own glory. Then you separate yourself from God and do yourself harm.

Your main question should always be whether something is lived with or without God. You have your own inner knowledge to answer that question. Every time you do something that comes from your needs for acceptance, affirmation, or affection, and every time you do something that makes these needs grow, you know that you are not with God. These needs will never be satisfied; they will only increase when you yield to them. But every time you do something for the glory of God, you will know God's peace in your heart and find rest there.

Rely on Your Spiritual Guides

It is far from easy to keep living where God is. Therefore, God gives you people who help to hold you in that place and call you back to it every time you wander off. Your spiritual guides keep reminding you of where your deepest desire is being fulfilled. You know where that is, but you distrust your own knowledge.

So rely on your spiritual guides. They may at times be stern and demanding or seem unrealistic, as though they are not considering all your needs. But it is when you lose your confidence in them that you are most vulnerable. As soon as you start saying to yourself, "My guides are getting bored with me; they talk about me without letting me in on their conversations; they treat me as a patient who should not be told everything about his condition," you are most susceptible to outside attacks.

Let nothing come between you and your spiritual guides. When you find yourself tempted to distrust them, let them know immediately so that they can prevent your imaginings from leading you further away from them, can restore your confidence in them, and can reaffirm their commitment to you.

Go into the Place of Your Pain

You have to live through your pain gradually and thus deprive it of its power over you. Yes, you must go into the place of your pain, but only when you have gained some new ground. When you enter your pain simply to experience it in its rawness, it can pull you away from where you want to go.

What is your pain? It is the experience of not receiving what you most need. It is a place of emptiness where you feel sharply the absence of the love you most desire. To go back to that place is hard, because you are confronted there with your wounds as well as with your powerlessness to heal yourself. You are so afraid of that place that you think of it as a place of death. Your instinct for survival makes you run away and go looking for something else that can give you a sense of at-homeness, even though you know full well that it can't be found out in the world.

You have to begin to trust that your experience of emptiness is not the final experience, that beyond it is a place where you are being held in love. As long as you do not trust that place beyond your emptiness, you cannot safely reenter the place of pain.

So you have to go into the place of your pain with the knowledge in your heart that you have already found the new place. You have already tasted some of its fruits. The more roots you have in the new place, the more capable you are of mourning the loss of the old place and letting go of the pain that lies there. You cannot mourn something that has not died. Still, the old pains, attachments, and desires that once meant so much to you need to be buried.

You have to weep over your lost pains so that they can gradually leave you and you can become free to live fully in the new place without melancholy or homesickness.

Open Yourself to the First Love

You have been speaking a lot about dying to old attachments in order to enter the new place, where God is waiting for you. But it is possible to end up with too many noes—no to your former way of thinking and feeling, no to things you did in the past, and most of all, no to human relationships that were once precious and life-giving. You are setting up a spiritual battle full of noes, and you work yourself to despair when you realize how hard it seems, if not impossible, to cut yourself off from the past.

The love that came to you in particular, concrete human friendships and that awakened your dormant desire to be completely and unconditionally loved was real and authentic. It does not have to be denied as dangerous and idolatrous. A love that comes to you through human beings is true, God-given love and needs to be celebrated as such. When human friendships prove to be unlivable because you demand that your friends love you in ways that are beyond human capacity, you do not have to deny the reality of the love you received. When you try to die to that love in order to find God's love, you are doing something God does not want. The task is not to die to life-giving relationships but to realize that the love you received in them is part of a greater love.

God has given you a beautiful self. There God dwells and loves you with the first love, which precedes all human love. You carry your own beautiful, deeply loved self in your heart. You can and must hold on to the truth of the love you were given and recognize that same love in others who see your goodness and love you.

So stop trying to die to the particular real love you have received. Be grateful for it and see it as what enabled you to open yourself to God's first love.

Acknowledge Your Powerlessness

There are places in you where you are completely powerless. You so much want to heal yourself, fight your temptations, and stay in control. But you cannot do it yourself. Every time you try, you are more discouraged. So you must acknowledge your powerlessness. This is the first step in Alcoholics Anonymous and the treatment of all addictions. You might as well think of your struggle this way. Your inexhaustible need for affection is an addiction. It rules your life and makes you a victim.

Simply start by admitting that you cannot cure yourself. You have to say yes fully to your powerlessness in order to let God heal you. But it is not really a question of *first* and *then.* Your willingness to experience your powerlessness already includes the beginning of surrender to God's action in you. When you cannot sense anything of God's healing presence, the acknowledgment of your powerlessness is too frightening. It is like jumping from a high wire without a net to catch you.

Your willingness to let go of your desire to control your life reveals a certain trust. The more you relinquish your stubborn need to maintain power, the more you will get in touch with the One who has the power to heal and guide you. And the more you get in touch with that divine power, the easier it will be to confess to yourself and to others your basic powerlessness.

One way you keep holding on to an imaginary power is by expecting something from outside gratifications or future events. As long as you run from where you are and distract yourself, you cannot fully let yourself be healed. A seed only flourishes by staying in the ground in which it is sown. When you keep digging the seed up to check whether it is growing, it will never bear fruit. Think about yourself as a little seed planted in rich soil. All you have to do is stay there and trust that the soil contains everything you need to grow. This growth takes place even when you do not feel it. Be quiet, acknowledge your powerlessness, and have faith that one day you will know how much you have received.

Seek a New Spirituality

You are beginning to realize that your body is given to you to affirm your self. Many spiritual writers speak about the body as if it cannot be trusted. This might be true if your body has not come home. But once you have brought your body home, once it is an integral part of your self, you can trust it and listen to its language.

When you find yourself curious about the lives of people you are with or filled with desires to possess them in one way or another, your body has not yet fully come home. As soon as you have come to live in your body as a true expression of who you are, your curiosity will vanish, and you will be present to others free from needs to know, or own.

A new spirituality is being born in you. Not body denying or body indulging but truly incarnational. You have to trust that this spirituality can find shape within you, and that it can find articulation through you. You will discover that many other spiritualities you have admired and tried to practice no longer completely fit your unique call. You will begin sensing when other people's experiences and ideas no longer match your own. You have to start trusting your unique vocation and allow it to grow deeper and stronger in you so it can blossom in your community.

As you bring your body home, you will be more able to discern with your whole being the value of other people's spiritual experiences and their conceptualization. You will be able to understand and appreciate them without desiring to imitate them. You will be more self-confident and free to claim your unique place in life as God's gift to you. There will be no need for comparisons. You will walk your own way, not in isolation but with the awareness that you do not have to worry whether others are pleased or not.

Look at Rembrandt and van Gogh. They trusted their vocations and did not allow anyone to lead them astray. With true Dutch stubbornness, they followed their vocations from the moment they recognized them. They didn't bend over backward to please their friends or enemies. Both ended their lives in poverty, but both left humanity with gifts that could heal the minds and hearts of many generations of people. Think of these two men and trust that you too have a unique vocation that is worth claiming and living out faithfully.

Tell Your Story in Freedom

The years that lie behind you, with all their struggles and pains, will in time be remembered only as the way that led to your new life. But as long as the new life is not fully yours, your memories will continue to cause you pain. When you keep reliving painful events of the past, you can feel victimized by them. But there is a way of telling your story that does not create pain. Then, also, the need to tell your story will become less pressing. You will see that you are no longer there: the past is gone, the pain has left you, you no longer have to go back and relive it, you no longer depend on your past to identify yourself.

There are two ways of telling your story. One is to tell it compulsively and urgently, to keep returning to it because you see your present suffering as the result of your past experiences. But there is another way. You can tell your story from the place where it no longer dominates you. You can speak about it with a certain distance and see it as the way to your present freedom. The compulsion to tell your story is gone. From the perspective of the life you now live and the distance you now have, your past does not loom over you. It has lost its weight and can be remembered as God's way of making you more compassionate and understanding toward others.

Find the Source of
Your Loneliness

Whenever you feel lonely, you must try to find the source of this feeling. You are inclined either to run away from your loneliness or to dwell in it. When you run away from it, your loneliness does not really diminish; you simply force it out of your mind temporarily. When you start dwelling in it, your feelings only become stronger, and you slip into depression.

The spiritual task is not to escape your loneliness, not to let yourself drown in it, but to find its source. This is not so easy to do, but when you can somehow identify the place from which these feelings emerge, they will lose some of their power over you. This identification is not an intellectual task; it is a task of the heart. With your heart you must search for that place without fear.

This is an important search because it leads you to discern something good about yourself. The pain of your loneliness may be rooted in your deepest vocation. You might find that your loneliness is linked to your call to live completely for God. Thus your loneliness may be revealed to you as the other side of your unique gift. Once you can experience in your innermost being the truth of this, you may find your loneliness not only tolerable but even fruitful. What seemed primarily painful may then become a feeling that, though painful, opens for you the way to an even deeper knowledge of God's love.

Keep Returning to the Road
to Freedom

When suddenly you seem to lose all you thought you had gained, do not despair. Your healing is not a straight line. You must expect setbacks and regressions. Don't say to yourself, "All is lost. I have to start all over again." This is not true. What you have gained, you have gained.

Sometimes little things build up and make you lose ground for a moment. Fatigue, a seemingly cold remark, someone's inability to hear you, someone's innocent forgetfulness, which feels like rejection—when all these come together, they can make you feel as if you are right back where you started. But try to think about it instead as being pulled off the road for a while. When you return to the road, you return to the place where you left it, not to where you started.

It is important not to dwell on the small moments when you feel pulled away from your progress. Try to return home, to the solid place within you, immediately. Otherwise, these moments start connecting with similar moments, and together they become powerful enough to pull you far away from the road. Try to remain alert to seemingly innocuous distractions. It is easier to return to the road when you are on the shoulder than when you are pulled all the way into a nearby swamp.

In everything, keep trusting that God is with you, that God has given you companions on the journey. Keep returning to the road to freedom.

Let Jesus Transform You

You are looking for ways to meet Jesus. You are trying to meet him not only in your mind but also in your body. You seek his affection, and you know that this affection involves his body as well as yours. He became flesh for you so that you could encounter him in the flesh and receive his love in the flesh.

But something remains in you that prevents this meeting. There is still a lot of shame and guilt stuck away in your body, blocking the presence of Jesus. You do not fully feel at home in your body; you look down on it as if it were not a good enough, beautiful enough, or pure enough place to meet Jesus.

When you look attentively at your life, you will see how filled it has been with fears, especially fears of people in authority: your parents, your teachers, your bishops, your spiritual guides, even your friends. You never felt equal to them and kept putting yourself down in front of them. For most of your life, you have felt as if you needed their permission to be yourself.

Think about Jesus. He was totally free before the authorities of his time. He told people not to be guided by the behavior of the scribes and Pharisees.

Jesus came among us as an equal, a brother. He broke down the pyramidal structures of relationship between God and people as well as those among people and offered a new model: the circle, where God lives in full solidarity with the people and the people with one another.

You will not be able to meet Jesus in your body while your body remains full of doubts and fears. Jesus came to free you from these bonds and to create in you a space where you can be with him. He wants you to live the freedom of the children of God.

Do not despair, thinking that you cannot change yourself after so many years. Simply enter into the presence of Jesus as you are and ask him to give you a fearless heart where he can be with you. *You* cannot make yourself different. *Jesus* came to give you a new heart, a new spirit, a new mind, and a new body. Let him transform you by his love and so enable you to receive his affection in your whole being.

Befriend Your Emotions

It can be discouraging to discover how quickly you lose your inner peace. Someone who happens to enter your life can suddenly create restlessness and anxiety in you. Sometimes this feeling is there before you fully realize it. You thought you were centered; you thought you could trust yourself; you thought you could stay with God. But then someone you do not even know intimately makes you feel insecure. You ask yourself whether you are loved or not, and that stranger becomes the criterion. Thus you start feeling disillusioned by your own reaction.

Don't whip yourself for your lack of spiritual progress. If you do, you will easily be pulled even further away from your center. You will damage yourself and make it more difficult to come home again. It is obviously good not to act on your sudden emotions. But you don't have to repress them, either. You can acknowledge them and let them pass by. In a certain sense, you have to befriend them so that you do not become their victim.

The way to "victory" is not in trying to overcome your dispiriting emotions directly but in building a deeper sense of safety and at-homeness and a more incarnate knowledge that you are deeply loved. Then, little by little, you will stop giving so much power to strangers.

Do not be discouraged. Be sure that God will truly fulfill all your needs. Keep remembering that. It will help you not to expect that fulfillment from people who you already know are incapable of giving it.

Follow Your Deepest Calling

When you discover in yourself something that is a gift from God, you have to claim it and not let it be taken away from you. Sometimes people who do not know your heart will altogether miss the importance of something that is part of your deepest self, precious in your eyes as well as God's. They might not know you well enough to be able to respond to your genuine needs. It is then that you have to speak your heart and follow your own deepest calling.

There is a part of you that too easily gives in to others' influence. As soon as someone questions your motives, you start doubting yourself. You end up agreeing with the other before you have consulted your own heart. Thus you grow passive and simply assume that the other knows better.

Here you have to be very attentive to your inner self. "Coming home" and "being given back to yourself" are expressions that indicate that you have a solid inner base from which you can speak and act—without apologies—humbly but convincingly.

Remain Anchored in Your Community

When your call to be a compassionate healer gets mixed up with your need to be accepted, the people you want to heal will end up pulling you into their world and robbing you of your healing gift. But when, out of fear of becoming a person who suffers, you fail to get close to such people, you cannot reach them and restore them to health. You feel deeply the loneliness, alienation, and spiritual poverty of your contemporaries. You want to offer them a truly healing response that comes from your faith in the Gospel. But often you have found yourself hooked by curiosity and a need for affection, and so you have lost the ability to bring the good news to those to whom you came so close.

It is important to remain as much in touch as possible with those who know you, love you, and protect your vocation. If you visit people with great needs and deep struggles that you can easily recognize in your own heart, remain anchored in your home community. Think about your community as holding a long line that girds your waist. Wherever you are, it holds that line. Thus you can be very close to people in need of your healing without losing touch with those who protect your vocation. Your community can pull you back when its members see that you are forgetting why you were sent out.

When you feel a burgeoning need for sympathy, support, affection, and care from those to whom you are being sent, remember that there is a place where you can receive those gifts in a safe and responsible way. Do not let yourself be seduced by the dark powers that imprison those you want to set free. Keep returning to those to whom you belong and who keep you in the light. It is that light that you desire to bring into the darkness. You do not have to fear anyone as long as you remain safely anchored in your community. Then you can carry the light far and wide.

Stay with Your Pain

When you experience the deep pain of loneliness, it is understandable that your thoughts go out to the person who was able to take that loneliness away, even if only for a moment. When, underneath all the praise and acclaim, you feel a huge absence that makes everything look useless, your heart wants only one thing—to be with the person who once was able to dispel these frightful emotions. But it is the absence itself, the emptiness within you, that you have to be willing to experience, not the one who could temporarily take it away.

It is not easy to stay with your loneliness. The temptation is to nurse your pain or to escape into fantasies about people who will take it away. But when you can acknowledge your loneliness in a safe, contained place, you make your pain available for God's healing.

God does not want your loneliness; God wants to touch you in a way that permanently fulfills your deepest need. It is important that you dare to stay with your pain and allow it to be there. You have to own your loneliness and trust that it will not always be there. The pain you suffer now is meant to put you in touch with the place where you most need healing, your very heart. The person who was able to touch that place has revealed to you your pearl of great price.

It is understandable that everything you did, are doing, or plan to do seems completely meaningless compared with that pearl. That pearl is the experience of being fully loved. When you experience deep loneliness, you are willing to give up everything in exchange for healing. But no human being can heal that pain. Still, people will be sent to you to mediate God's healing, and they will be able to offer you the deep sense of belonging that you desire and that gives meaning to all you do.

Dare to stay with your pain, and trust in God's promise to you.

Live Patiently with the "Not Yet"

A part of you was left behind very early in your life: the part that never felt completely received. It is full of fears. Meanwhile, you grew up with many survival skills. But you want your self to be one. So you have to bring home the part of you that was left behind. That is not easy, because you have become quite a formidable person, and your fearful part does not know if it can safely dwell with you. Your grown-up self has to become very childlike—hospitable, gentle, and caring—so your anxious self can return and feel safe.

You complain that it is hard for you to pray, to experience the love of Jesus. But Jesus dwells in your fearful, never fully received self. When you befriend your true self and discover that it is good and beautiful, you will see Jesus there. Where you are most human, most yourself, weakest, there Jesus lives. Bringing your fearful self home is bringing Jesus home.

As long as your vulnerable self does not feel welcomed by you, it keeps so distant that it cannot show you its true beauty and wisdom. Thus, you survive without really living.

Try to keep your small, fearful self close to you. This is going to be a struggle, because you have to live for a while with the "not yet." Your deepest, truest self is not yet home. It quickly gets scared. Since your intimate self does not feel safe with you, it continues to look for others, especially those who offer it some real, though temporary, consolation. But when you become more childlike, it will no longer feel the need to dwell elsewhere. It will begin to look to *you* as home.

Be patient. When you feel lonely, stay with your loneliness. Avoid the temptation to let your fearful self run off. Let it teach you its wisdom; let it tell you that you can live instead of just surviving. Gradually you will become one, and you will find that Jesus is living in your heart and offering you all you need.

Keep Moving Toward
Full Incarnation

Do not discount what you have already accomplished. You have made important steps toward the freedom you are searching for. You have decided to dedicate yourself completely to God, to make Jesus the center of your life, and to be fashioned into an instrument of God's grace. Yes, you still experience your inner dividedness, your need for approval and acclaim. But you see that you have made important choices that show where you want to go.

You can look at your life as a large cone that becomes narrower the deeper you go. There are many doors in that cone that give you chances to leave the journey. But you have been closing these doors one after the other, making yourself go deeper and deeper into your center. You know that Jesus is waiting for you at the end, just as you know that he is guiding you as you move in that direction. Every time you close another door—be it the door of immediate satisfaction, the door of distracting entertainment, the door of busyness, the door of guilt and worry, or the door of self-rejection—you commit yourself to go deeper into your heart and thus deeper into the heart of God.

This is a movement toward full incarnation. It leads you to become what you already are—a child of God; it lets you embody more and more the truth of your being; it makes you claim the God within you. You are tempted to think that you are a nobody in the spiritual life and that your friends are far beyond you on the journey. But this is a mistake.

You must trust the depth of God's presence in you and live from there. This is the way to keep moving toward full incarnation.

See Yourself Truthfully

You continue struggling to see your own truth. When people who know your heart well and love you dearly say that you are a child of God, that God has entered deeply into your being, and that you are offering much of God to others, you hear these statements as pep talks. You don't believe that these people are really seeing what they are saying.

You have to start seeing yourself as your truthful friends see you. As long as you remain blind to your own truth, you keep putting yourself down and referring to everyone else as better, holier, and more loved than you are. You look up to everyone in whom you see goodness, beauty, and love because you do not see any of these qualities in yourself. As a result, you begin leaning on others without realizing that you have everything you need to stand on your own feet.

You cannot force things, however. You cannot *make* yourself see what others see. You cannot fully claim yourself when parts of you are still wayward. You have to acknowledge where you are and affirm

that place. You have to be willing to live your loneliness, your incompleteness, your lack of total incarnation fearlessly, and trust that God will give you the
people to keep showing you the truth of who you
are.

Receive All the Love That Comes to You

While you may feel physically and mentally strong, you still experience a forceful undercurrent of anguish. You sleep well, you work well, but there are few waking moments when you do not feel that throbbing pain in your heart that makes everything seem up in the air. You know that you are progressing, but you can't understand why this anguish keeps pervading everything you think, say, or do. There is still a deep, unresolved pain, but you cannot take it away yourself. It exists far deeper than you can reach.

Be patient and trust. You have to move gradually deeper into your heart. There is a place far down that is like a turbulent river, and that place frightens you. But do not fear. One day it will be quiet and peaceful.

You have to keep moving, as you are doing. Live a faithful, disciplined life, a life that gives you a sense of inner strength, a life in which you can receive more and more of the love that comes to you. Wherever there is real love for you, take it and be strengthened by it. As your body, heart, and mind come to know that you are loved, your weakest part will feel attracted to that love. What has remained separated and unreachable will let itself be drawn into the love you have been able to receive. One day you will discover that your anguish is gone. It will leave you because your weakest self let itself be embraced by your love.

You are not yet there, but you are moving fast. There will be a bit more pain and struggle. You have to dare to live through it. Keep walking straight. Acknowledge your anguish, but do not let it pull you out of yourself. Hold on to your chosen direction, your discipline, your prayer, your work, your guides, and trust that one day love will have conquered enough of you that even the most fearful part will allow love to cast out all fear.

Stay United with the Larger Body

Your own growth cannot take place without growth in others. You are part of a body. When you change, the whole body changes. It is very important for you to remain deeply connected with the larger community to which you belong.

It is also important that those who belong to the body of which you are part keep faith in your journey. You still have a way to go, and there will be times when your friends are puzzled or even disillusioned by what is happening to you. At certain moments things may seem more difficult for you than before; they may look worse than when you began. You still have to make the great passage, and that might not happen without a lot of new distress and fear. Through all of this, it is important for you to stay united with the larger body and know that your journey is made not just for yourself but for all who belong to the body.

Think about Jesus. He made his journey and asked his disciples to follow him even where they would rather not go. The journey you are choosing is

Jesus' journey, and whether or not you are fully aware of it, you are also asking your brothers and sisters to follow you. Somewhere you already know that what you are living now will not leave the other members of the community untouched. Your choices also call your friends to make new choices.

Love Deeply

Do not hesitate to love and to love deeply. You might be afraid of the pain that deep love can cause. When those you love deeply reject you, leave you, or die, your heart will be broken. But that should not hold you back from loving deeply. The pain that comes from deep love makes your love ever more fruitful. It is like a plow that breaks the ground to allow the seed to take root and grow into a strong plant. Every time you experience the pain of rejection, absence, or death, you are faced with a choice. You can become bitter and decide not to love again, or you can stand straight in your pain and let the soil on which you stand become richer and more able to give life to new seeds.

The more you have loved and have allowed yourself to suffer because of your love, the more you will be able to let your heart grow wider and deeper. When your love is truly giving and receiving, those whom you love will not leave your heart even when they depart from you. They will become part of your self and thus gradually build a community within you.

Those you have deeply loved become part of you.

The longer you live, there will always be more people to be loved by you and to become part of your inner community. The wider your inner community becomes, the more easily you will recognize your own brothers and sisters in the strangers around you. Those who are alive within you will recognize those who are alive around you. The wider the community of your heart, the wider the community around you. Thus the pain of rejection, absence, and death can become fruitful. Yes, as you love deeply the ground of your heart will be broken more and more, but you will rejoice in the abundance of the fruit it will bear.

Stand Erect in Your Sorrow

The question is "Can you stand erect in your pain, your loneliness, your fears, and your experience of being rejected?" The danger is that you will be swept off your feet by these feelings. They will be here for a long time, and they will go on tempting you to be drowned in them. But you are called to acknowledge them and feel them while remaining on your feet.

Remember, Mary stood under the cross. She suffered her sorrow standing. Remember, Jesus spoke about the cosmic disasters and the glorious appearance of the Son of Man and said to his disciples, "When these things begin to take place, stand erect, hold your heads high, because your liberation is near at hand" (Luke 2:28). Remember, Peter and John cured the crippled man who was begging at the temple entrance. Peter said to him, "In the name of Jesus Christ the Nazarene, walk!" (Acts 3:6). Then he took him by the right hand and helped him to stand up.

You have to dare to stand erect in your struggles. The temptation is to complain, to beg, to be overwhelmed and find your satisfaction in the pity you evoke. But you know already that this is not gaining

61

for you what your heart most desires. As long as you remain standing, you can speak freely to others, reach out to them, and receive from them. Thus you speak and act from your center and invite others to speak and act from theirs. In this way, real friendships are possible and real community can be formed. God gives you the strength to stand in your struggles and to respond to them standing.

Let Deep Speak to Deep

When you "love" someone or "miss" someone, you experience an inner pain. Bit by bit you have to discover the nature of this pain. When your deepest self is connected with the deepest self of another, that person's absence may be painful, but it will lead you to a profound communion with the person, because loving each other is loving in God. When the place where God dwells in you is intimately connected with the place where God dwells in the other, the absence of the other person is not destructive. On the contrary, it will challenge you to enter more deeply into communion with God, the source of all unity and communion among people.

It is also possible on the other hand that the pain of absence will show you that you are out of touch with your own deeper self. You need the other to experience inner wholeness, to have a sense of well-being. You have become emotionally dependent on the other and sink into depression because of his or her absence. It feels as if the other has taken away a part of you that you cannot live without. Then the pain of absence reveals a certain lack of trust in God's love. But God is enough for you.

True love between two human beings puts you more in touch with your deepest self. It is a love *in* God. The pain you experience from the death or absence of the person you love, then, always calls you to a deeper knowledge of God's love. God's love is all the love you need, and it reveals to you the love of God in the other. So the God in you can speak to the God in the other. This is deep speaking to deep, a mutuality in the heart of God, who embraces both of you.

Death or absence does not end or even diminish the love of God that brought you to the other person. It calls you to take a new step into the mystery of God's inexhaustible love. This process is painful, very painful, because the other person has become a true revelation of God's love for you. But the more you are stripped of the God-given support of people, the more you are called to love God for God's sake. This is an awesome and even dreadful love, but it is the love that offers eternal life.

Allow Yourself to Be
Fully Received

Giving yourself to others without expecting anything in return is only possible when you have been fully received. Every time you discover that you expect something in return for what you have given or are disappointed when nothing comes back to you, you are being made aware that you yourself are not yet fully received. Only when you know yourself as unconditionally loved—that is, fully received—by God can you give gratuitously. Giving without wanting anything in return is trusting that all your needs will be provided for by the One who loves you unconditionally. It is trusting that you do not need to protect your own security but can give yourself completely to the service of others.

Faith is precisely trusting that you who give gratuitously will receive gratuitously, but not necessarily from the person to whom you gave. The danger is in pouring yourself out to others in the hope that *they* will fully receive you. You will soon feel as if others are walking away with parts of you. You cannot give yourself to others if you do not own yourself, and you can only truly own yourself when you have been fully received in unconditional love.

A lot of giving and receiving has a violent quality, because the givers and receivers act more out of need than out of trust. What looks like generosity is actually manipulation, and what looks like love is really a cry for affection or support. When you know yourself as fully loved, you will be able to give according to the other's capacity to receive, and you will be able to receive according to the other's capacity to give. You will be grateful for what is given to you without clinging to it, and joyful for what you can give without bragging about it. You will be a free person, free to love.

Claim Your Unique Presence in Your Community

Your unique presence in your community is the way God wants you to be present to others. Different people have different ways of being present. You have to know and claim your way. That is why discernment is so important. Once you have an inner knowledge of your true vocation, you have a point of orientation. That will help you decide what to do and what to let go of, what to say and what to remain silent about, when to go out and when to stay home, who to be with and who to avoid.

When you get exhausted, frustrated, overwhelmed, or run down, your body is saying that you are doing things that are none of your business. God does not require of you what is beyond your ability, what leads you away from God, or what makes you depressed or sad. God wants you to live for others and to live that presence well. Doing so might include suffering, fatigue, and even moments of great physical or emotional pain, but none of this must ever pull you away from your deepest self and God.

You have not yet fully found your place in your community. Your way of being present to your community may require times of absence, prayer, writing, or solitude. These too are times for your community. They allow you to be deeply present to your people and speak words that come from God in you. When it is part of your vocation to offer your people a vision that will nurture them and allow them to keep moving forward, it is crucial that you give yourself the time and space to let that vision mature in you and become an integral part of your being.

Your community needs you, but maybe not as a constant presence. Your community might need you as a presence that offers courage and spiritual food for the journey, a presence that creates the safe ground in which others can grow and develop, a presence that belongs to the matrix of the community. But your community also needs your creative absence.

You might need certain things that the community cannot provide. For these you may have to go elsewhere from time to time. This does not mean that you are selfish, abnormal, or unfit for community life. It means that your way of being present to your people necessitates personal nurturing of a special kind. Do not be afraid to ask for these things. Doing so allows you to be faithful to your vocation and to feel safe. It is a service to those for whom you want to be a source of hope and a life-giving presence.

Accept Your Identity as a Child of God

Your true identity is as a child of God. This is the identity you have to accept. Once you have claimed it and settled in it, you can live in a world that gives you much joy as well as pain. You can receive the praise as well as the blame that comes to you as an opportunity for strengthening your basic identity, because the identity that makes you free is anchored beyond all human praise and blame. You belong to God, and it is as a child of God that you are sent into the world.

You need spiritual guidance; you need people who can keep you anchored in your true identity. The temptation to disconnect from that deep place in you where God dwells and to let yourself be drowned in the praise or blame of the world always remains.

Since that deep place in you where your identity as a child of God is rooted has been unknown to you for a long time, those who were able to touch you there had a sudden and often overwhelming power over you. They became part of your identity. You could no longer live without them. But they could not fulfill that divine role, so they left you, and you felt abandoned. But it is precisely that experience of abandonment that called you back to your true identity as a child of God.

Only God can fully dwell in that deepest place in you and give you a sense of safety. But the danger remains that you will let other people run away with your sacred center, thus throwing you into anguish.

It might take a great deal of time and discipline to fully reconnect your deep, hidden self and your public self, which is known, loved, and accepted but also criticized by the world. Gradually, though, you will begin feeling more connected and become more fully who you truly are—a child of God. There lies your real freedom.

Own Your Pain

You wonder whether it is good to share your struggles with others, especially with those to whom you are called to minister. You find it hard not to mention your own pains and sorrows to those you are trying to help. You feel that what belongs to the core of your humanity should not be hidden. You want to be a fellow traveler, not a distant guide.

The main question is "Do you own your pain?" As long as you do not own your pain—that is, integrate your pain into your way of being in the world—the danger exists that you will use the other to seek healing for yourself. When you speak to others about your pain without fully owning it, you expect something from them that they cannot give. As a result, you will feel frustrated, and those you wanted to help will feel confused, disappointed, or even further burdened.

But when you fully own your pain and do not expect those to whom you minister to alleviate it, you can speak about it in true freedom. Then sharing your struggle can become a service; then your openness about yourself can offer courage and hope to others.

For you to be able to share your struggle as a service, it is also essential to have people to whom you can go with your own needs. You will always need safe people to whom you can pour out your heart. You will always need people who do not need you but who can receive you and give you back to yourself. You will always need people who can help you own your pain and claim your struggle.

Thus the core question in your ministry is "Is my sharing of my struggle in the service of the one who seeks my help?" This question can only be answered yes when you truly own your pain and expect nothing from those who seek your ministry.

Know Yourself as Truly Loved

Some people have lived such oppressed lives that their true selves have become completely unreachable to them. They need help to break through their oppression. Their power to free themselves has to be at least as strong as the power that keeps them down. Sometimes they need permission to explode: to let out their deepest emotions and to shake off the alien forces. Screaming, yelling, crying, and even physical fighting might be expressions of liberation.

You, however, do not seem to need such explosion. For you, the problem is not to get something *out* of your system but to take something *in* that deepens and strengthens your sense of your goodness and allows your anguish to be embraced by love.

You will discover that the more love you can take in and hold on to, the less fearful you will become. You will speak more simply, more directly, and more freely about what is important to you, without fear of other people's reactions. You will also use fewer words, trusting that you communicate your true self even when you do not speak much.

The disciples of Jesus had a real sense of his loving presence as they went out to preach. They had seen him, eaten with him, and spoken with him after his resurrection. They had come to live a deep connectedness with him and drew from that connectedness the strength to speak out with simplicity and directness, unafraid of being misunderstood or rejected.

The more you come to know yourself—spirit, mind, and body—as truly loved, the freer you will be to proclaim the good news. That is the freedom of the children of God.

Protect Your Innocence

Being a child of God does not make you free from temptations. You might have moments when you feel so blessed, so *in* God, so loved that you forget you are still living in a world of powers and principalities. But your innocence as a child of God needs to be protected. Otherwise, you will easily be pulled out of your true self and experience the devastating force of the darkness surrounding you.

This being pulled out may come as a great surprise. Before you are even fully aware of it or have had a chance to consent to it, you may find yourself overwhelmed by lust, anger, resentment, or greed. A picture, a person, or a gesture may trigger these strong, destructive emotions and seduce your innocent self.

As a child of God, you need to be prudent. You cannot simply walk around in this world as if nothing and no one can harm you. You remain extremely vulnerable. The same passions that make you love God may be used by the powers of evil.

The children of God need to support, protect, and hold one another close to God's heart. You belong to a minority in a large, hostile world. As you become more aware of your true identity as a child of God, you will also see more clearly the many forces that try to convince you that all things spiritual are false substitutes for the real things of life.

When you are temporarily pulled out of your true self, you can have the sudden feeling that God is just a word, prayer is fantasy, sanctity is a dream, and the eternal life is an escape from true living. Jesus was tempted in this way, and so are we.

Do not trust your thoughts and feelings when you are pulled out of yourself. Return quickly to your true place, and pay no attention to what tricked you. Gradually you will come to be more prepared for these temptations, and they will have less and less power over you. Protect your innocence by holding on to the truth: you are a child of God and deeply loved.

Let Your Lion Lie Down
with Your Lamb

There is within you a lamb and a lion. Spiritual maturity is the ability to let lamb and lion lie down together. Your lion is your adult, aggressive self. It is your initiative-taking and decision-making self. But there is also your fearful, vulnerable lamb, the part of you that needs affection, support, affirmation, and nurturing.

When you heed only your lion, you will find yourself overextended and exhausted. When you take notice only of your lamb, you will easily become a victim of your need for other people's attention. The art of spiritual living is to fully claim both your lion and your lamb. Then you can act assertively without denying your own needs. And you can ask for affection and care without betraying your talent to offer leadership.

Developing your identity as a child of God in no way means giving up your responsibilities. Likewise, claiming your adult self in no way means that you cannot become increasingly a child of God. In fact, the opposite is true. The more you can feel safe as a child of God, the freer you will be to claim your mission in the world as a responsible human being. And the more you claim that you have a unique task to fulfill for God, the more open you will be to letting your deepest need be met.

The kingdom of peace that Jesus came to establish begins when your lion and your lamb can freely and fearlessly lie down together.

Be a Real Friend

Friendship has been a source of great pain for you. You desired it so much that you often lost yourself in the search for a true friend. Many times you became desperate when a friendship you hoped for didn't materialize, or when a friendship begun with great expectations did not last.

Many of your friendships grew from your need for affection, affirmation, and emotional support. But now you must seek friends to whom you can relate from your center, from the place where you know that you are deeply loved. Friendship becomes more and more possible when you accept yourself as deeply loved. Then you can be with others in a non-possessive way. Real friends find their inner correspondence where both know the love of God. There spirit speaks to spirit and heart to heart.

True friendships are lasting because true love is eternal. A friendship in which heart speaks to heart is a gift from God, and no gift that comes from God is temporary or occasional. All that comes from God participates in God's eternal life. Love between people, when given by God, is stronger than death. In this sense, true friendships continue beyond the boundary of death. When you have loved deeply, that love can grow even stronger after the death of the person you love. That is the core message of Jesus.

When Jesus died, the disciples' friendship with him did not diminish. On the contrary, it grew. This is what the sending of the Spirit was all about. The Spirit of Jesus made Jesus' friendship with his disciples everlasting, stronger and more intimate than before his death. That is what Paul experienced when he said, "It is no longer I, but Christ living in me" (Galatians 2:20).

You have to trust that every true friendship has no end, that a communion of saints exists among all those, living and dead, who have truly loved God and one another. You know from experience how real this is. Those you have loved deeply and who have died live on in you, not just as memories but as real presences.

Dare to love and to be a real friend. The love you give and receive is a reality that will lead you closer and closer to God as well as to those whom God has given you to love.

Trust Your Friends

You keep looking for proof of friendship, but in doing so you harm yourself. When you give something to your friends, do not keep waiting for a concrete response, a thank-you. When you really believe that you are loved by God, you can allow your friends the freedom to respond to your love in *their* way. They have their own histories, their own characters, their own ways of receiving love. They may be slower, more hesitant, or more cautious than you. They may want to be with you in ways that are real and authentic for them but unusual for you. Trust that those who love you want to show you their love in a real way, even when their choices of time, place, and form are different from yours.

Much of your ability to trust your friends depends on your belief in your own goodness. When you give a gift freely and spontaneously, do not worry about your motives. Don't say to yourself, "Maybe I gave this gift to get something in return. Maybe I gave this gift to force my friend into a closeness he or she does not want." Trust your intuitions.

Allow your friends the freedom to respond as they want and are able to. Let their receiving be as free as your giving. Then you will become capable of feeling true gratitude.

Control Your Own Drawbridge

You must decide for yourself to whom and when you give access to your interior life. For years you have permitted others to walk in and out of your life according to *their* needs and desires. Thus you were no longer master in your own house, and you felt increasingly used. So, too, you quickly became tired, irritated, angry, and resentful.

Think of a medieval castle surrounded by a moat. The drawbridge is the only access to the interior of the castle. The lord of the castle must have the power to decide when to draw the bridge and when to let it down. Without such power, he can become the victim of enemies, strangers, and wanderers. He will never feel at peace in his own castle.

It is important for you to control your own drawbridge. There must be times when you keep your bridge drawn and have the opportunity to be alone or only with those to whom you feel close. Never allow yourself to become public property, where anyone can walk in and out at will. You might think that you are being generous in giving access to anyone who wants to enter or leave, but you will soon find yourself losing your soul.

When you claim for yourself the power over your drawbridge, you will discover new joy and peace in your heart and find yourself able to share that joy and peace with others.

Avoid All Forms of
Self-Rejection

You must avoid not only blaming others but also blaming yourself. You are inclined to blame yourself for the difficulties you experience in relationships. But self-blame is not a form of humility. It is a form of self-rejection in which you ignore or deny your own goodness and beauty.

When a friendship does not blossom, when a word is not received, when a gesture of love is not appreciated, do not blame it on yourself. This is both untrue and hurtful. Every time you reject yourself, you idealize others. You want to be with those whom you consider better, stronger, more intelligent, more gifted than yourself. Thus you make yourself emotionally dependent, leading others to feel unable to fulfill your expectations and causing them to withdraw from you. This makes you blame yourself even more, and you enter a dangerous spiral of self-rejection and neediness.

Avoid all forms of self-rejection. Acknowledge

your limitations, but claim your unique gifts and thereby live as an equal among equals. That will set you free from your obsessive and possessive needs and enable you to give and receive true affection and friendship.

Take Up Your Cross

Your pain is deep, and it won't just go away. It is also uniquely yours, because it is linked to some of your earliest life experiences.

Your call is to bring that pain home. As long as your wounded part remains foreign to your adult self, your pain will injure you as well as others. Yes, you have to incorporate your pain into your self and let it bear fruit in your heart and the hearts of others.

This is what Jesus means when he asks you to take up your cross. He encourages you to recognize and embrace your unique suffering and to trust that your way to salvation lies therein. Taking up your cross means, first of all, befriending your wounds and letting them reveal to you your own truth.

There is great pain and suffering in the world. But the pain hardest to bear is your own. Once you have taken up that cross, you will be able to see clearly the crosses that others have to bear, and you will be able to reveal to them their own ways to joy, peace, and freedom.

Keep Trusting God's Call

As you come to realize that God is beckoning you to a greater hiddenness, do not be afraid of that invitation. Over the years you have allowed the voices that call you to action and great visibility to dominate your life. You still think, even against your own best intuitions, that you need to do things and be seen in order to follow your vocation. But you are now discovering that God's voice is saying, "Stay home, and trust that your life will be fruitful even when hidden."

It is not going to be easy to listen to God's call. Your insecurity, your self-doubt, and your great need for affirmation make you lose trust in your inner voice and run away from yourself. But you know that God speaks to you through your inner voice and that you will find joy and peace only if you follow it. Yes, your spirit is willing to follow, but your flesh is weak.

You have friends who know that your inner voice speaks the truth and who can affirm what it says. They offer you the safe space where you can let that voice become clearer and louder. There will be people who will tell you that you are wasting your time and talents, that you are fleeing from true responsibility, that you fail to use the influence you have. But don't let yourself be misled. They do not speak in God's name. Trust the few who know your inner journey and want you to be faithful to it. They will help you stay faithful to God's call.

Claim the Victory

You are still afraid to die. That fear is connected with the fear that you are not loved. Your question "Do you love me?" and your question "Do I have to die?" are deeply connected. You asked these questions as a little child, and you are still asking them.

As you come to know that you are loved fully and unconditionally, you will also come to know that you do not have to fear death. Love is stronger than death; God's love was there for you before you were born and will be there for you after you have died.

Jesus has called you from the moment you were knitted together in your mother's womb. It is your vocation to receive and give love. But from the very beginning you have experienced the forces of death. They attacked you all through your years of growing up. You have been faithful to your vocation even though you have often felt overwhelmed by darkness. You know now that these dark forces will have no final power over you. They seem overwhelming, but the victory is already won. It is the victory of Jesus, who has called you. He overcame for you the power of death so that you could live in freedom.

You have to claim that victory and not live as if

death still controlled you. Your soul knows about the victory, but your mind and emotions have not fully accepted it. They go on struggling. In this respect you remain a person of little faith. Trust the victory and let your mind and emotions gradually be converted to the truth. You will experience new joy and new peace as you let that truth reach every part of your being. Don't forget: victory has been won, the powers of darkness no longer rule, love is stronger than death.

Face the Enemy

As you see more clearly that your vocation is to be a witness to God's love in this world, and as you become more determined to live out that vocation, the attacks of the enemy will increase. You will hear voices saying, "You are worthless, you have nothing to offer, you are unattractive, undesirable, unlovable." The more you sense God's call, the more you will discover in your own soul the cosmic battle between God and Satan. Do not be afraid. Keep deepening your conviction that God's love for you is enough, that you are in safe hands, and that you are being guided every step of the way. Don't be surprised by the demonic attacks. They will increase, but as you face them without fear, you will discover that they are powerless.

What is important is to keep clinging to the real, lasting, and unambiguous love of Jesus. Whenever you doubt that love, return to your inner spiritual home and listen there to love's voice. Only when you know in your deepest being that you are intimately loved can you face the dark voices of the enemy without being seduced by them.

The love of Jesus will give you an ever-clearer

vision of your call as well as of the many attempts to pull you away from that call. The more you are called to speak for God's love, the more you will need to deepen the knowledge of that love in your own heart. The farther the outward journey takes you, the deeper the inward journey must be. Only when your roots are deep can your fruits be abundant. The enemy is there, waiting to destroy you, but you can face the enemy without fear when you know that you are held safe in the love of Jesus.

Continue Seeking Communion

A desire for communion has been part of you since you were born. The pain of separation, which you experienced as a child and continue to experience now, reveals to you this deep hunger. All your life you have searched for a communion that would break your fear of death. This desire is sincere. Don't look on it as an expression of your neediness or as a symptom of your neurosis. It comes from God and is part of your true vocation.

Nonetheless, your fear of abandonment and rejection is so intense that your search for communion is often replaced by a longing for concrete expressions of friendship or affection. You want deep communion, but you end up looking for invitations, letters, phone calls, gifts, and similar gestures. When these do not come in the way you wish, you start distrusting even your deep desire for communion. Your search for communion often takes place too far from where true communion can be found.

Still, communion is your authentic desire, and it will be given to you. But you have to dare to stop seeking gifts and favors like a petulant child and trust that your deepest longing will be fulfilled. Dare to lose your life and you will find it. Trust in Jesus' words: "There is no one who has left house, brothers, sisters, mother, father, children or land for my sake and for the sake of the gospel who will not receive a hundred times as much, houses, brothers, sisters, mothers, children and land—and persecutions too—now in this present time and, in the world to come, eternal life" (Mark 10:29–30).

Separate the False Pains from the Real Pain

There is a real pain in your heart, a pain that truly belongs to you. You know now that you cannot avoid, ignore, or repress it. It is this pain that reveals to you how you are called to live in solidarity with the broken human race.

You must distinguish carefully, however, between your pain and the pains that have attached themselves to it but are not truly yours. When you feel rejected, when you think of yourself as a failure and a misfit, you must be careful not to let these feelings and thoughts pierce your heart. You are not a failure or a misfit. Therefore, you have to disown these pains as false. They can paralyze you and prevent you from loving the way you are called to love.

It is a struggle to keep distinguishing the real pain from the false pains. But as you are faithful to that struggle, you will see more and more clearly your unique call to love. As you see that call, you will be more and more able to claim your real pain as your unique way to glory.

Say Often, "Lord, Have Mercy"

You wonder what to do when you feel attacked on all sides by seemingly irresistible forces, waves that cover you and want to sweep you off your feet. Sometimes these waves consist of feeling rejected, feeling forgotten, feeling misunderstood. Sometimes they consist of anger, resentment, or even the desire for revenge, and sometimes of self-pity and self-rejection. These waves make you feel like a powerless child abandoned by your parents.

What are you to do? Make the conscious choice to move the attention of your anxious heart away from these waves and direct it to the One who walks on them and says, "It's me. Don't be afraid" (Matthew 14:27; Mark 6:50; John 6:20). Keep turning your eyes to him and go on trusting that he will bring peace to your heart. Look at him and say, "Lord, have mercy." Say it again and again, not anxiously but with confidence that he is very close to you and will put your soul to rest.

Let God Speak Through You

You are confronted again and again with the choice of letting God speak or letting your wounded self cry out. Although there has to be a place where you can allow your wounded part to get the attention it needs, your vocation is to speak from the place in you where God dwells.

When you let your wounded self express itself in the form of apologies, arguments, or complaints—through which it cannot be truly heard—you will only grow frustrated and increasingly feel rejected. Claim the God, in you, and let God speak words of forgiveness, healing, and reconciliation, words calling to obedience, radical commitment, and service.

People will constantly try to hook your wounded self. They will point out your needs, your character defects, your limitations and sins. That is how they attempt to dismiss what God, through you, is saying to them. Your temptation, arising from your great insecurity and doubt, is to begin believing their definition of you. But God has called you to speak the Word to the world and to speak it fearlessly. While acknowledging your woundedness, do not let go of the truth that lives in you and demands to be spoken.

It will take a great deal of time and patience to distinguish between the voice of your wounded self and the voice of God, but as you grow more and more faithful to your vocation, this will become easier. Do not despair; you are being prepared for a mission that will be hard but fruitful.

Know That You Are Welcome

Not being welcome is your greatest fear. It connects with your birth fear, your fear of not being welcome in this life, and your death fear, your fear of not being welcome in the life after this. It is the deep-seated fear that it would have been better if you had not lived.

Here you are facing the core of the spiritual battle. Are you going to give in to the forces of darkness that say you are not welcome in this life, or can you trust the voice of the One who came not to condemn you but to set you free from fear? You have to choose for life. At every moment you have to decide to trust the voice that says, "I love you. I knit you together in your mother's womb" (Psalm 139:13).

Everything Jesus is saying to you can be summarized in the words "Know that you are welcome." Jesus offers you his own most intimate life with the Father. He wants you to know all he knows and to do all he does. He wants his home to be yours. Yes, he wants to prepare a place for you in his Father's house.

Keep reminding yourself that your feelings of being unwelcome do not come from God and do not tell the truth. The Prince of Darkness wants you to believe that your life is a mistake and that there is no home for you. But every time you allow these thoughts to affect you, you set out on the road to self-destruction. So you have to keep unmasking the lie and think, speak, and act according to the truth that you are very, very welcome.

Permit *Your* Pain to Become *the* Pain

Your pain, deep as it is, is connected with specific circumstances. You do not suffer in the abstract. You suffer because someone hurts you at a specific time and in a specific place. Your feelings of rejection, abandonment, and uselessness are rooted in the most concrete events. In this way all suffering is unique. This is eminently true of the suffering of Jesus. His disciples left him, Pilate condemned him, Roman soldiers tortured and crucified him.

Still, as long as you keep pointing to the specifics, you will miss the full meaning of your pain. You will deceive yourself into believing that if the people, circumstances, and events had been different, your pain would not exist. This might be partly true, but the deeper truth is that the situation which brought about your pain was simply the form in which you came in touch with the human condition of suffering. Your pain is the concrete way in which you participate in the pain of humanity.

Paradoxically, therefore, healing means moving from *your* pain to *the* pain. When you keep focusing on the specific circumstances of your pain, you easily become angry, resentful, and even vindictive. You are inclined to do something about the externals of your pain in order to relieve it; this explains why you often seek revenge. But real healing comes from realizing that your own particular pain is a share in humanity's pain. That realization allows you to forgive your enemies and enter into a truly compassionate life. That is the way of Jesus, who prayed on the cross: "Father forgive them; they do not know what they are doing" (Luke 23:34). Jesus' suffering, concrete as it was, was the suffering of all humanity. *His* pain was *the* pain.

Every time you can shift your attention away from the external situation that caused your pain and focus on the pain of humanity in which you participate, your suffering becomes easier to bear. It becomes a "light burden" and an "easy yoke" (Matthew 11:30). Once you discover that you are called to live in solidarity with the hungry, the homeless, the prisoners, the refugees, the sick, and the dying, your very personal pain begins to be converted into *the* pain and you find new strength to live it. Herein lies the hope of all Christians.

Give Your Agenda to God

You are very concerned with making the right choices about your work. You have so many options that you are constantly overwhelmed by the question "What should I do and what should I not do?" You are asked to respond to many concrete needs. There are people to visit, people to receive, people to simply be with. There are issues that beg for attention, books it seems important to read, and works of art to be seen. But what of all this truly deserves your time?

Start by not allowing these people and issues to possess you. As long as you think that you need them to be yourself, you are not really free. Much of their urgency comes from your own need to be accepted and affirmed. You have to keep going back to the source: God's love for you.

In many ways, you still want to set your own agenda. You act as if you have to choose among many things, which all seem equally important. But you have not fully surrendered yourself to God's guidance. You keep fighting with God over who is in control.

Try to give your agenda to God. Keep saying,

"Your will be done, not mine." Give every part of your heart and your time to God and let God tell you what to do, where to go, when and how to respond. God does not want you to destroy yourself. Exhaustion, burnout, and depression are not signs that you are doing God's will. God is gentle and loving. God desires to give you a deep sense of safety in God's love. Once you have allowed yourself to experience that love fully, you will be better able to discern who you are being sent to in God's name.

It is not easy to give your agenda to God. But the more you do so, the more "clock time" becomes "God's time," and God's time is always the fullness of time.

Let Others Help You Die

You are so afraid of dying alone. Your deeply hidden memories of a fearful birth make you suspect that your death will be equally fearful. You want to be sure that you won't cling to your present existence but will have the inner freedom to let go and trust that something new will be given to you. You know that only someone who truly loves you can help you link this life with the next.

But maybe the death you fear is not simply the death at the end of your present life. Maybe the death at the end of your life won't be so fearful if you can die well now. Yes, the real death—the passage from time into eternity, from the transient beauty of this world to the lasting beauty of the next, from darkness into light—has to be made now. And you do not have to make it alone.

God has sent people to be very close to you as you gradually let go of the world that holds you captive. You must trust fully in their love. Then you will never feel completely alone. Even though no one can do it for you, you can make the lonely passage in the knowledge that you are surrounded by a safe love and that those who let you move away from them will be there to welcome you on the other side. The more you trust in the love of those God has sent to you, the more you will be able to lose your life and so gain it.

Success, notoriety, affection, future plans, entertainment, satisfying work, health, intellectual stimulation, emotional support—yes, even spiritual progress—none of these can be clung to as if they are essential for survival. Only as you let go of them can you discover the true freedom your heart most desires. That is dying, moving into the life beyond life. You must make that passage now, not just at the end of your earthly life. You cannot do it alone, but with the love of those who are being sent to you, you can surrender your fear and let yourself be guided into the new land.

Live Your Wounds Through

You have been wounded in many ways. The more you open yourself to being healed, the more you will discover how deep your wounds are. You will be tempted to become discouraged, because under every wound you uncover you will find others. Your search for true healing will be a suffering search. Many tears still need to be shed.

But do not be afraid. The simple fact that you are more aware of your wounds shows that you have sufficient strength to face them.

The great challenge is *living* your wounds through instead of *thinking* them through. It is better to cry than to worry, better to feel your wounds deeply than to understand them, better to let them enter into your silence than to talk about them. The choice you face constantly is whether you are taking your hurts to your head or to your heart. In your head you can analyze them, find their causes and consequences, and coin words to speak and write about them. But no final healing is likely to come from that source. You need to let your wounds go down into your heart. Then you can live them through and discover that they will not destroy you. Your heart is greater than your wounds.

Understanding your wounds can only be healing when that understanding is put at the service of your heart. Going to your heart with your wounds is not easy; it demands letting go of many questions. You want to know "Why was I wounded? When? How? By whom?" You believe that the answers to these questions will bring relief. But at best they only offer you a little distance from your pain. You have to let go of the need to stay in control of your pain and trust in the healing power of your heart. There your hurts can find a safe place to be received, and once they have been received, they lose their power to inflict damage and become fruitful soil for new life.

Think of each wound as you would of a child who has been hurt by a friend. As long as that child is ranting and raving, trying to get back at the friend, one wound leads to another. But when the child can experience the consoling embrace of a parent, she or he can live through the pain, return to the friend, forgive, and build up a new relationship. Be gentle with yourself, and let your heart be your loving parent as you live your wounds through.

For Now, Hide Your Treasure

You have found a treasure: the treasure of God's love. You know now where it is, but you are not yet ready to own it fully. So many attachments keep pulling you away. If you would fully own your treasure, you must hide it in the field where you found it, go off happily to sell everything you own, and then come back and buy the field.

You can be truly happy that you have found the treasure. But you should not be so naive as to think that you already own it. Only when you have let go of everything else can the treasure be completely yours. Having found the treasure puts you on a new quest for it. The spiritual life is a long and often arduous search for what you have already found. You can only seek God when you have already found God. The desire for God's unconditional love is the fruit of having been touched by that love.

Because finding the treasure is only the beginning of the search, you have to be careful. If you expose the treasure to others without fully owning it, you might harm yourself and even lose the treasure. A newfound love needs to be nurtured in a quiet, intimate space. Overexposure kills it. That is why you must hide the treasure and spend your energy in selling your property so that you can buy the field where you have hidden it.

This is often a painful enterprise, because your sense of who you are is so intimately connected to all the things you own: success, friends, prestige, money, degrees, and so on. But you know that nothing but the treasure itself can truly satisfy you. Finding the treasure without being ready yet to fully own it will make you restless. This is the restlessness of the search for God. It is the way to holiness. It is the road to the kingdom. It is the journey to the place where you can rest.

Keep Choosing God

You are constantly facing choices. The question is whether you choose for God or for your own doubting self. You know what the right choice is, but your emotions, passions, and feelings keep suggesting you choose the self-rejecting way.

The root choice is to trust at all times that God is with you and will give you what you most need. Your self-rejecting emotions might say, "It isn't going to work. I'm still suffering the same anguish I did six months ago. I will probably fall back into the old depressive patterns of acting and reacting. I haven't really changed." And on and on. It is hard not to listen to these voices. Still, you know that these are not God's voice. God says to you, "I love you, I am with you, I want to see you come closer to me and experience the joy and peace of my presence. I want to give you a new heart and a new spirit. I want you to speak with my mouth, see with my eyes, hear with my ears, touch with my hands. All that is mine is yours. Just trust me and let me be your God."

This is the voice to listen to. And that listening requires a real choice, not just once in a while but every moment of each day and night. It is you who decides what you think, say, and do. You can think yourself into a depression, you can talk yourself into low self-esteem, you can act in a self-rejecting way. But you always have a choice to think, speak, and act in the name of God and so move toward the Light, the Truth, and the Life.

As you conclude this period of spiritual renewal, you are faced once again with a choice. You can choose to remember this time as a failed attempt to be completely reborn, or you can also choose to remember it as the precious time when God began new things in you that need to be brought to completion. Your future depends on how you decide to remember your past. Choose for the truth of what you know. Do not let your still anxious emotions distract you. As you keep choosing God, your emotions will gradually give up their rebellion and be converted to the truth in you.

You are facing a real spiritual battle. But do not be afraid. You are not alone. Those who have guided you during this period are not leaving you. Their prayers and support will be with you wherever you go. Keep them close to your heart so that they can guide you as you make your choices.

Remember, you are held safe. You are loved. You are protected. You are in communion with God and with those whom God has sent you. What is of God will last. It belongs to the eternal life. Choose it, and it will be yours.

Conclusion

Today, the period in which I wrote these spiritual imperatives seems far away and long ago. Reading them now, eight years later, makes me aware of the radical changes I have undergone. I have moved through anguish to freedom, through depression to peace, through despair to hope. It certainly was a time of purification for me. My heart, ever questioning my goodness, value, and worth, has become anchored in a deeper love and thus less dependent on the praise and blame of those around me. It also has grown into a greater ability to give love without always expecting love in return.

None of this happened suddenly. In truth, the weeks and months following my self-imposed exile were so difficult that I wondered at first if anything had changed at all. I tiptoed around my community, always afraid of getting caught again in the old emotional traps. But gradually, hardly perceptibly, I discovered that I was no longer the person who had left the community in despair. I discovered this not so much in myself but in those who, instead of being embarrassed by what I had gone through, gave me their confidence and trust. Most of all, I found new confidence in myself through the gradual renewal of the friendship that had triggered my anguish. Never had I dared to believe that this broken relationship could be healed. But as I kept claiming for myself the truth of my freedom as a child of God, endowed with an abundance of love, my obsessive needs melted away and a true mutuality became possible.

This does not mean that there are no longer tensions or conflicts, or that moments of desolation, fear, anger, jealousy, or resentment are completely absent. There is hardly a day without some dark clouds drifting by. But today I recognize them for what they are without putting my head in them!

I have also learned to catch the darkness early, not to allow sadness to grow into depression or let a sense of being rejected develop into a feeling of abandonment. Even in the renewed and deepened friendship, I feel the freedom to point to the little clouds and ask for help in letting them pass by.

What once seemed such a curse has become a blessing. All the agony that threatened to destroy my life now seems like the fertile ground for greater trust, stronger hope, and deeper love.

I am not a young man anymore. Still, I may have quite a few years left to live. Can I live them gracefully and joyfully, continuing to profit from what I learned in my exile? I certainly desire to do so. During my months of anguish, I often wondered if God is real or just a product of my imagination. I now know that while I felt completely abandoned, God didn't leave me alone. Many friends and family members have died during the past eight years, and my own death is not so far away. But I have heard the inner voice of love, deeper and stronger than ever. I want to keep trusting in that voice and be led by it beyond the boundaries of my short life, to where God is all in all.